# To Kill a Mockingbird:

## *A Reader's Guide to the Harper Lee Novel*

ROBERT CRAYOLA

# CONTENTS

# INTRODUCTION

Harper Lee's *To Kill a Mockingbird* has been viewed as a classic almost from the moment of its release in 1960. Thanks in part to the film version released just two years after the book, the story has reached an enormous amount of people, with sales estimated at around 30 million by 2014. It is continually taught in schools, and characters like Atticus Finch and Boo Radley sound familiar even to people who haven't read the book.

In this guide we'll be looking at the book in great detail, exploring the context and origins of the story, and sorting out the plot so we can get a deeper understanding of the book's themes and meaning. I will be revealing all major plot details, so if you don't want spoilers, go and read the book first.

**AUTHOR:** Let's begin our study with a look at the author of *To Kill a Mockingbird*, Harper Lee.

Nelle Harper Lee (born April 28, 1926) has a great deal in common with Scout Finch, the narrator of *To Kill a Mockingbird*. Her father was in the Alabama State Legislature and also served as a lawyer, even defending two black men in a case.

Lee grew up in Monroeville, Alabama, a small town

like Maycomb in her novel. She was a tomboy like Scout and had a friend similar to Dill – the young Truman Capote, who went on to become a respected author in his own right with stories like *Breakfast at Tiffany's* and *In Cold Blood*.

Unlike Scout, however, Lee's mother was alive to raise her, and Lee had four older siblings.

Lee had a strong interest in reading and writing in high school. She went to Huntingdon College in Montgomery and began to write stories. She wrote the early draft of *To Kill a Mockingbird*, and she revised it for a few years. She was able to get it published in 1960, and it immediately proved to be a success both critically and commercially.

Since its publication, Lee has published no other books, only a few short nonfiction pieces. She assisted Truman Capote in his research for *In Cold Blood* (as depicted in the film *Capote*), but has primarily chosen to live a private life.

**CONTEXT:** Lee published her novel at a time when racial segregation was being strongly contested, and blacks struggled for equal rights. Although written by a Southerner, Lee was not afraid to criticize her fellow Southerners, while also showing the good things about the South. She presented complex issues from the perspective of a child. Nevertheless, the book has been (and continues to be) challenged for its depiction of rape and use of racial slurs.

# THE ELEMENTS OF LITERATURE

**WHAT KIND OF BOOK IS THIS?:** The book is a novel of standard length.

**STRUCTURE:** The book is divided into two sections, totaling 31 chapters. The first section focuses on establishing the setting and has a more childlike feel. The second section has more conflict and deals with more adult issues.

**SETTING:** Nearly all of the book takes place in Maycomb, Alabama, a small town based on Harper Lee's childhood home of Monroeville, Alabama. Because Maycomb is so small, most of the people seem to have at least a passing familiarity with each other. Also, because the town is far from other towns, it has an isolated feel, like a self-contained world.

**NARRATOR AND P.O.V.:** The narrator is Scout Finch, a woman looking back on her childhood. Although it's unclear how much Scout understands as a child about rape and the racial issues taking place, she presents them clearly and the reader can understand what she refers to.

Scout is a headstrong young woman, a tomboy, with a strong moral compass and a great deal of courage that helps her follow her heart.

**TENSE:** The book is written in the past tense.

**TONE:** Tone is how a book "feels." Although it is written as a woman looking back on her childhood, much of the book expresses the view of a girl who is new to many things in the world. Yet even though she is largely inexperienced with many things, there is a boldness, curiosity, and intelligence to her observations.

**PLOT:** The plot is the book's story. Here is a quick snapshot of the plot. We'll take a deeper look in the chapter summaries.

An intelligent young girl named Scout narrates the story of a few years time. She has a brother named Jem and a father named Atticus, who is a lawyer. The children befriend a neighbor boy named Dill and become fascinated with a mysterious man named Boo Radley, who is never seen outside his house.

Atticus takes a court case defending a black man named Tom Robinson, accused of raping a white woman, Mayella Ewell. Atticus loses the case, but shames her father Bob Ewell in the process. Bob Ewell vows revenge.

Tom Robinson is killed while allegedly trying to escape from prison. Bob Ewell attempts to attack Scout and Jem as they come home from a Halloween pageant. They are able to make their escape with the help of Boo Radley. Bob Ewell dies from his own knife mysteriously, and Boo seems to be responsible. Scout escorts him home, reflecting on her growth and Boo's desire for isolation.

**PROTAGONIST:** The protagonist is the main character or characters that we most sympathize with.

Scout is the main protagonist, but Jem and Atticus are also significant protagonists.

**ANTAGONIST:** The antagonist opposes the protagonists. Bob Ewell is most clearly the antagonist, Racism and mob mentality can also be viewed as antagonizing forces.

**CONFLICT:** Conflict is the struggle faced by the characters. It increases throughout the novel as Scout realizes that her father's decision to defend a black man has made him greatly disliked among some members of the town. Bob Ewell becomes more of a physical threat to the protagonists later in the novel.

**CLIMAX:** The climax is the moment of greatest tension in the story. This occurs as Scout and Jem are walking home from the pageant and Bob Ewell tries to attack them.

**RESOLUTION:** The resolution is how the story concludes after the climax has passed. Once the children are safe from Bob Ewell, Jem recovers at home, Scout and the others clarify what actually occurred, and Boo Radley receives their gratitude for saving the children's' lives.

**BOOK TITLE:** The book title refers to something Atticus says to Jem when the boy is given a gun. Atticus tells him: "Remember it's a sin to kill a mockingbird." The reason, according to a neighbor, is that mockingbirds just make music and don't hurt anyone. This connects to characters like Tom Robinson and Boo Radley, who are innocent, but attacked by the outside world in various ways. In a larger sense, it also refers to the theme of racism and justice.

**THEMES:** Themes are what the author chooses to illustrate through the narrative. Some of the themes in the novel include:

*Coming of age, maturity*

*Community interactions, connections, and standards*

*Racism*

*Justice and compassion*

*The Southern lifestyle (particularly in small towns)*

*Class and hierarchy*

*Gender roles*

# CHARACTERS

**JEAN LOUISE "SCOUT" FINCH** – Scout is the narrator and main protagonist. She is the daughter of Atticus and the brother of Jem. She is a girl just entering school in the beginning of the book, but starts to have the maturity of a young woman by the end. She is a tomboy, intelligent, with a great deal of courage to stand up for what she believes in.

**ATTICUS FINCH** – Atticus is the father of Scout and Jem. He is an older man whose wife died several years earlier. He works as a lawyer and will defend Tom Robinson in the trial that makes up a great part of the book. He has a strong moral compass and sense of compassion that he will impart to his children.

**JEREMY ATTICUS "JEM" FINCH** – Jem is Scout's older brother and the son of Atticus. He is close to Scout throughout the book, but because he is four years older and more mature, he starts to keep her at some distance. He struggles to remain polite in the face of the townspeople's treatment toward his father.

**CHARLES BAKER "DILL" HARRIS** – Dill is a neighbor boy who Scout and Jem quickly befriend. He visits in the summer and stays with his aunt Rachel. He is adopted by a family who he doesn't feel close to and runs away to visit Scout and Jem. Dill is very interested in Boo Radley.

**CALPURNIA** – Calpurnia is the black cook and caretaker of Jem and Scout. In the absence of a mother, she is the closest thing they have. She will take the children to visit her church.

**ARTHUR "BOO" RADLEY** – Boo is a mysterious figure who had a troubled youth and is now a neighborhood recluse. The children are intensely curious about him. Boo will help save their lives at the end of the novel.

**TOM ROBINSON** – Tom is a black man accused of raping a white woman. He stands trial and is defended by Atticus. Tom is convicted and later shot down.

**BOB EWELL** – Ewell is the father of Mayella, the woman who accuses Tom Robinson of raping her. The Ewells are notorious as "white trash" and Bob Ewell is infamous for being a lazy drunk.

**MAYELLA EWELL** – Mayella accuses Tom Robinson of rape, but Atticus implies that it was really her father who raped her and that Tom Robinson is a scapegoat. Mayella has led a rough life, and she readily agrees to say whatever her father tells her.

**AUNT ALEXANDRA** – Atticus's sister, the aunt of Jem and Scout, comes to stay with them during the trial to lend the Finch house an air of respectability and to teach the children (particularly Scout) how to be genteel.

**MISS MAUDIE ATKINSON** – Maudie is a neighbor and good friend of the Finch household. She is not afraid to speak her mind, however unpopular her opinions might be. Like Atticus, she has a strong moral compass and sense of justice.

**MRS. HENRY LAFAYETTE DUBOSE** – This is

another neighbor. She is elderly and dying and trying to overcome morphine addiction. She is particularly mean-spirited with what she says, and this finally causes Jem to destroy her flowers. He reads to the old woman to make amends for his deed.

**NATHAN RADLEY** – Boo's older brother. He is more visible in the neighborhood and plugs up the tree where the children found random items.

**MISS RACHEL HAVERFORD** – Dill's aunt and a neighbor of the Finches.

**MISS STEPHANIE CRAWFORD** – A neighbor of the Finches known for gossiping.

**HECK TATE** – Heck is the sheriff of Maycomb.

**LINK DEAS** – Tom Robinson's employer. He tries to help Tom in court and later help Tom's wife.

**HELEN ROBINSON** – Tom Robinson's wife.

**MR. UNDERWOOD** – The publisher of the town newspaper. An outspoken man who tries to help Atticus.

**BURRIS EWELL** – A son of Bob Ewell. He is in Scout's class for a day and then drops out.

**REVEREND SYKES** – The pastor at Calpurnia's church. He also sits with Jem and Scout at the trial.

**MR. DOLPHUS RAYMOND** – A white man who has married a black woman. He pretends to be drunk to account for his behavior.

**MR. WALTER CUNNINGHAM** – A poor farmer Atticus has done some legal work for. He is part of a mob that wants to take Tom Robinson from jail to kill him. He is largely responsible for the mob turning away.

**WALTER CUNNINGHAM** – A boy in Scout's class. Initially she beats him up, but later she treats him more kindly.

**UNCLE JACK FINCH** – The brother of Atticus and Aunt Alexandra. He punishes Scout and then regrets it, realizing there is a lot he doesn't know about children.

**FRANCIS HANCOCK** – This is a relative of Scout's who taunts her, inciting her to do violence against Francis.

**JUDGE JOHN TAYLOR** – He presides over Tom Robinson's trial.

**MR. HORACE GILMER** – The attorney who represents Mayella Ewell.

**MISS CAROLINE FISHER** – Scout's first teacher at school.

**MISS GATES** – Scout's second teacher.

**EULA MAY** – The telephone operator.

# CHAPTER SUMMARIES & COMMENTARY

## PART ONE

**CHAPTER 1:** The book begins with a great deal of *exposition* – the author's way of filling the reader in on things that happened before the events in the book. We learn from Scout, the narrator, that she is a young girl living with her father Atticus and her brother Jem. They have a black maid named Calpurnia, and they're living in Maycomb, a small town in Alabama. The opening sentence is "When he was nearly thirteen, my brother Jem got his arm badly broken at the elbow." The whole book is going to lead up to that incident, and it'll take so long to occur that we're likely to forget about it, the way it was so casually mentioned.

Scout explains that her father is a lawyer with a long family history. Scout and Jem's mother died of a heart attack when Scout was only two, so she doesn't remember her. The book begins when she is six and Jem is almost ten. It's summertime and there is a new arrival in the neighborhood – a boy named Dill. Jem and Scout quickly warm up to him when he tells them about his trips to the movies (especially *Dracula*), and they're good friends after that.

Jem and Scout tell Dill about the Radley Place, a house in their neighborhood with strange, almost mythical inhabitants. Boo Radley, a man who supposedly only comes out at night, will be rumored and hinted at throughout the book. He mixed with a bad crowd when he was a young man and after interference by law enforcement, seems to have been confined to the Radley house in the years since. His reputation is almost like that of a ghost, and Dill is intrigued. He dares Jem to touch the Radley house and Jem feels obligated to show he's not afraid. Jem reaches the house and runs away, and they think they see movement from the window of the house.

**CHAPTER 2:** The summer ends and Dill returns to Meridian (he was only visiting his aunt in Maycomb). Scout begins school – she's in the first grade and is very excited about going. Jem takes her but doesn't associate with her in the same way there.

Scout's teacher is Miss Caroline, who isn't very "street smart" with the Maycomb kids. Scout already knows how to read – she compares it to breathing, something she's always known how to do. Miss Caroline thinks that Atticus taught Scout to read and wants to begin her on material that's much too simple. Scout is punished for the way she talks and reads. She dislikes school quickly.

There's a boy in her class named Walter Cunningham. Atticus did some law work for his father. They are a poor family of farmers and they paid Atticus in potatoes and firewood. Miss Caroline tries to lend Walter a quarter to get lunch, but he refuses because he wouldn't be able to pay her back. Scout tells Miss Caroline this and the teacher is angry and hits Scout's hand with a ruler. Leaving for lunch, Scout thinks, "She was a pretty little thing." Scout is more of a tomboy and recognizes that Miss Caroline is more of a girly girl.

**CHAPTER 3:** Scout starts beating up Walter Cunningham in the schoolyard because she views him as the cause of her trouble. Jem stops Scout and invites Walter to their house for lunch (they call it *dinner*). They all eat with Atticus at the house and are served by Calpurnia. Scout has few social skills and says things that might embarrass Walter. Calpurnia scolds and corrects her, saying, "That boy's yo' comp'ny and if he wants to eat up the table cloth you let him, you hear?"

Now she feels slighted by Calpurnia. Atticus tells Scout that Calpurnia is an important part of the household and that she does a lot for Scout.

Scout returns to school and finds Miss Caroline screaming. A boy named Burris Ewell has "cooties" in his hair (presumably lice) and it unsettles her. Ironically, the children in the class aren't afraid at all. This only makes Miss Caroline look weaker. She tells the boy to go home and wash his hair. But the boy was going to leave anyway. He comes from a lowly family that most people in the book look down on. The Ewells will be part of an important trial later in the book. But for now we just get a hint that they are rude and poor. Burris Ewell says to Miss Caroline, "Ain't no snot-nosed slut of a schoolteacher ever born c'n make me do nothin'!" After the Ewell boy has left, the children comfort Miss Caroline. She has thin skin and is new to working with children.

On her way home, Scout resolves not to go back to school — she doesn't like that she has to learn to read again in some strange way. Calpurnia greets her when she gets home and tells Scout that she missed her. Feeling miserable, Scout finally tells Atticus about her day at school. Atticus asks her to see things from Miss Caroline's point of view. They finally agree to have Scout keep going to school, but they will continue to read at night. They'll keep it a secret. Atticus says, "...I have a feeling that if you tell Miss Caroline we read every night she'll get after *me*." Atticus is always looking for a peaceful solution, and this is the first of many instances where he takes a slow, cautionary course of action.

**CHAPTER 4:** Scout's first school year progresses and she is overall dissatisfied with school. One day while walking home, Scout discovers some tin foil and chewing gum inside a tree on the Radley lot. She shows Jem and he tells her to spit out the gum. He's more cautious and fearful about anything found on the Radley lot. Later, Scout shows Jem the tree and they discover some pennies inside. They try to determine who might have put the things there and think it might be someone's hiding place, but then decide that they can keep anything left there.

Summer arrives and the children are out of school. Dill returns to town (he's in Mississippi the rest of the year). As they play games, Scout is rolled in a tire and ends up at the Radley house. They are still frightened and fascinated by that house and role-play a game involving the Radleys. Atticus sees them and suspects what they are up to, chastises them. Scout remembers that when she rolled into the Radley yard in the tire, she heard laughing from inside the house.

**CHAPTER 5:** Much of the summer is spent with the children playing on the lawn of a neighbor, Miss Maudie Atkinson, who loves being outdoors, and loves her flowers. They question her about Boo Radley, who they suspect is dead, but she denies this. "Arthur [Boo] Radley just stays in the house, that's all," she says.

We also see in Miss Maudie how people live their religion in different ways. She follows the spirit of what she thinks is right, not necessarily the word of the law. Because Scout and Jem have people like Atticus and Miss Maudie to act as examples of morality, they aren't as subject to the mindless "popular" morality of much of the town.

The children decide to leave a note for Boo Radley, asking him to come out sometime. They're not able to deliver it successfully however, and Atticus asks them what they were doing. When he learns they tried to get Boo to come out, Atticus tells them to leave the man alone. Atticus makes it sound like they were making fun of Boo, and the children are both peeved and embarrassed by Atticus's accusation.

**CHAPTER 6:** On Dill's last night in town that summer, the children make their way to the Radley house. They want to have a peek inside. Scout cautions them against it, but they are determined to get a look at Boo Radley. To get into the backyard, they go through a tight wire fence. They make some noise and a man comes out toward them. They flee and Jem gets his pants caught on the wire fence. In the rush to escape, Jem leaves the pants behind. They return to the street and try to act casual, and find a group of neighbors in front of the Radley house, where Mr. Radley had shot his gun at what he believed was a black man in his collard green plants. They notice that Jem isn't wearing pants, and Dill quickly lies about winning them from Jem in a game of strip poker.

After returning home, Jem decides to go back and look for his pants on the fence. Scout thinks he's crazy and that he'll be killed by Mr. Radley. But Jem is able to secure the pants without incident, and without Atticus knowing that he left the house.

**CHAPTER 7:** Scout starts the second grade in this chapter and she likes it even less than the first. Jem has been moody and finally tells Scout that when he went back to get his pants that night, they were neatly folded across the fence like someone knew he'd be coming back for them. Along with the found items in the tree, the event adds to the general spookiness of Boo Radley, the natural suspect for the deed. They go by the tree where they'd found items before and discover a ball of twine. They think they're gifts of some sort. Scout reports: "From then on, we considered everything we found in the knot-hole our property."

One day, they pass the tree and discover two small figures carved in soap. They depict a boy and a girl and they realize that the figures are meant to be Jem and Scout. They think of everyone they know who carves, but none of the suspects seem likely. Later, they find a pocket watch. They decide to write a letter to whoever is leaving the items in the tree, but when they next go to it, they find that the hole's been sealed up with cement. They ask Mr. Radley if he did it, and he confirms that he did. "Tree's dying," he says. "You plug 'em with cement when they're sick."

Jem questions Atticus if the tree is really dying, and Atticus says it looks healthy enough. But when Jem tells him what Mr. Radley said, Atticus changes his tune and says that Mr. Radley probably knows more about it than he does.

Jem and Scout are suspicious of the whole business and naturally don't believe Mr. Radley's explanation for sealing up the tree.

**CHAPTER 8:** Winter sets in and it's the coldest one since 1885. Old Mrs. Radley dies, and Jem and Scout want to know if Atticus saw Arthur (Boo) Radley when he went to their house – he did not.

It begins to snow, something Scout and Jem have never seen. They get to take off school and play in the snow. That night as Scout sleeps, Atticus wakes her and Jem to take them outside. Miss Maudie Atkinson's house has caught fire and Atticus fears it might spread to their house. Men struggle to get the fire truck to Miss Maudie's house in the cold. People are removing furniture from the house. The fire spreads to the Finch house, but the firemen are able to extinguish it. Miss Maudie's house is not so fortunate. It collapses.

Atticus returns to his children and discovers Scout has a blanket on her shoulders. He is angry with her for leaving to get it, but she denies this and they realize that Boo Radley put it on her shoulders. This frightens Jem and he quickly admits everything that's happened between Boo and them – the hidden items in the tree, the pants neatly folded across the fence, etc. The children view Boo Radley more positively now – less like an evil ghost and more like a benevolent spirit that helps them in mysterious ways.

Miss Maudie seems hardly dismayed by her destroyed house. She is glad to have more space in her yard (or at least she puts on a happy face about it). Miss Maudie is depicted as a good and optimistic person throughout the book, and like Atticus, a model for Scout to look up to.

**CHAPTER 9:** At Scout's school, a boy named Cecil Jacobs tells her that her father "defended niggers," and this makes Scout lose her cool. She wants to fight the boy but remembers a promise to Atticus not to fight anymore, so she can only yell. She later asks Atticus if it's true. He says it is, but asks Scout not to use the word "nigger." Atticus goes on to explain about the man he's defending, Tom Robinson. This court case will be the major thread that the book follows. He admits to Scout that he doesn't think he'll win the case, but he says he must try. He says: "Simply because we were licked a hundred years before we started is no reason for us not to try to win." However, he tells Scout that the people they're fighting are their friends and neighbors, and that she mustn't lose her temper with them. She agrees, and suffers being called a coward by Cecil Jacobs at school.

Christmas comes and Scout sees some extended family. They include Uncle Jack Finch, Atticus's brother, Aunt Alexandra, Uncle Jimmy, and Francis, a boy about Scout's age. They go to Finch's Landing on Christmas. Uncle Jack doesn't like the language Scout uses (using words like *damn* and *hell* to show Atticus the negative influence of school, which she still dislikes).

On Christmas, Scout and Jem get air rifles from Atticus. Scout tries to brag to Francis about her gifts, but she finds him generally annoying. He is getting on her nerves, and when he calls Atticus a "nigger-lover" it's too much for Scout to handle. She punches him. Uncle Jack interrupts and punishes her for it. She later criticizes his defense of Francis, not giving her a chance to explain herself. When she does say she was defending her father and that it was justified, Uncle Jack realizes he was in the wrong. Scout later hears Atticus and Uncle Jack talking about the difficulties Scout and Jem will have to endure as the Tom Robinson trial approaches. Then Atticus suddenly tells Scout to go to bed. He knew she was eavesdropping the whole time, and he wanted her to hear what he had to say.

**CHAPTER 10:** Jem is maturing and wants to do

things like play football and shoot his air rifle. He tries to get Atticus to play football with him, but Atticus says he is too old. This makes Jem and Scout think that their father isn't good at anything "manly."

One day, Scout and Jem see a dog on their street walking in a strange way. They tell Calpurnia. She looks at the dog and thinks it's a mad (rabid) dog, and thus very dangerous. She phones Atticus and everyone she can in the neighborhood. Atticus and the sheriff (Heck Tate) soon arrive and decide the dog must be shot so it won't attack anyone. The sheriff insists that Atticus do the shooting. After some hesitation, Atticus agrees. To Scout and Jem's surprise, their father shoots the dog accurately. They learn from the others that their father was once famous for his shooting ability.

Scout and Jem feel a newfound pride for their father. They realize he is humble, and Jem is inspired to behave more like his father. He says, "Atticus is a gentleman, just like me!"

**CHAPTER 11:** This chapter focuses on a neighbor, Mrs. Dubose. She lives alone with one servant and is very old and sick. Scout and Jem hate her for her meanness, and they can't pass her house without her yelling something at them. Jem and Scout try to ignore her cruel words, but it finally gets to Jem when she says, "Your father's no better than the niggers and trash he works for!"

Using a baton that he just bought Scout, Jem hacks away at Mrs. Dubose's plants, to Scout's horror. They go home to await Atticus, who soon arrives and tries to understand what led Jem to damage the old woman's plants like that. He explains that many people will say things about Atticus and that Jem and Scout will have to get used to it. "Atticus, you must be wrong," Jem says.

But Atticus doesn't think so, not in his heart. He says, "The one thing that doesn't abide by majority rule is a person's conscience."

Atticus makes Jem return to Mrs. Dubose's yard and clean up the mess he's made. She also demands that Jem read to her for a month. He obviously doesn't want to, but Atticus says he must.

He begins to go and read to the old woman. Scout goes to the woman's house with Jem. Old Mrs. Dubose is stern at first, but then she seems to not even be paying attention to them or the words Jem reads.

As Jem and Scout deal with a woman who would hurl abuse on their father, Atticus reminds them that she is sick. This will parallel Atticus's attitude toward the entire town. They verbally abuse him, but he only views them as "sick," and underneath that delusion he sees them as friends and neighbors. He refuses to hate them, and this is what he's trying to impart to Jem and Scout.

Mrs. Dubose dies, and Atticus explains that she had been a morphine addict – that Jem's reading helped her to kick the habit before she died.

She left a box with a flower in it for Jem. Jem thinks she is mocking him from the grave, but Atticus says otherwise: "I think that was her way of telling you – everything's all right now, Jem, everything's all right."

Something of this lesson seems to have reached Jem and Scout. Atticus adds: "I wanted you to see what real courage is, instead of getting the idea that courage is a man with a gun in his hand. It's when you know you're licked before you begin but you begin anyway and see it through no matter what."

That's the kind of courage Atticus will have to employ as the Tom Robinson case goes to trial.

# PART TWO

**CHAPTER 12:** Scout has begun to notice a change in Jem, who is now twelve. He has hit puberty and is trying to be more of a man. He's not as close to Scout as he used to be.

Summer has arrived but not Dill, who has foster parents. Also, Atticus is away at the state legislature on business, so Scout is a little sad and lonely. She talks with Calpurnia, who realizes as Sunday approaches that the children don't have anyone to take them to church. She decides to bring them to her own church and grooms the children so it reflects well on her.

Calpurnia's church is called First Purchase African M.E. Church and Jem and Scout are the only white people there. People eyeball the children, and one woman named Lula says to Calpurnia: "I wants to know why you bringin' white chillun to nigger church."

Lula tries to interfere more, but the other church members intervene and the rude woman is heard from no more. People recognize that Jem and Scout are Atticus's children, and Atticus is the man defending Tom Robinson. They respect him for that and welcome the children to their church.

The church experience is very different from what Jem and Scout are used to. There are no hymn books because most of the people there are illiterate (Calpurnia is a notable exception). Instead of reading the songs, a leader recites them and the audience repeats back.

Another occurrence Scout finds unusual is when collection is taken up. People make donations, but when the money is examined the Reverend announces that it's not enough. They need more money for Tom Robinson's wife, who cannot find work while Tom is in jail. A second collection is taken up until they have enough money.

After the service ends, Scout is curious about why Tom Robinson's wife can't work. Calpurnia tells Scout that it's because of what Tom Robinson has been charged with. Bob Ewell accused Robinson of raping his daughter. Scout isn't quite clear what rape is, and Calpurnia tells her to ask Atticus.

Scout finds the whole experience of visiting Calpurnia's church fascinating. It has made Scout more curious about Calpurnia, who she sees in a new light, and Scout asks if she might visit Calpurnia's home someday. Calpurnia gladly agrees. Like Atticus and Miss Maudie Atkinson, Calpurnia is a role model Scout can look up to.

As Scout and the others arrive home, they discover Aunt Alexandra (Atticus's sister) waiting for them on the porch.

**CHAPTER 13:** They speak with their aunt and learn that she will be staying with them for an unspecified amount of time. She tells them the reason is to have some "feminine influence" upon them. Scout suspects that there is a deeper reason for her aunt's visit. When Atticus gets home, he tells Scout, "Your aunt's doing me a favor as well as you all. I can't stay here all day with you, and the summer's going to be hot one." Aunt Alexandra's presence seems like an attempt to remind people of gentility and manners. Since Atticus is involved with a controversial trial, he wants to make sure people remain polite around his family.

The neighbors do welcome Aunt Alexandra, although Scout is less than thrilled about her aunt. The woman keeps trying to turn Scout into a polite young lady. Scout is a tomboy and will have none of it, and because Scout is an intelligent person she is good at arguing with her aunt in a way that appears rude to the woman.

This chapter takes the opportunity to explain Maycomb society in more detail. Because of the geographical nature of the town, it is largely cut off from the outside world, and everyone seems to be related to everyone else. There is a neighborly quality to it that isn't found in larger cities.

Atticus tries to convince Jem and Scout to listen to their aunt and act in a more genteel manner, but Scout starts to cry and Jem says, "Atticus, is all this behavin' an' stuff gonna make things different?"

Realizing the foolhardiness of his words, Atticus takes a step back and tell his children to forget about it. Even though he is grateful to Alexandra for being there with them, Atticus is also determined to let the children be true to themselves. We see in this scene that even though Atticus is set up as a wise and moral character, he still makes mistakes and learns from them like other people. This gives him a humanity that makes us respect him even more.

**CHAPTER 14:** Jem and Scout are discussed by townspeople within their hearing, and Scout hears someone say, "They c'n go loose and rape up the countryside for all of 'em who run this county care," and she asks Atticus what rape is. He gives her a very academic definition, and it's unclear how much of it she understands.

Scout reveals the details of their trip to Calpurnia's church. Atticus is amused but Alexandra is not. Scout is confused by the whole matter. Alexandra thinks Calpurnia's services should be eliminated altogether, but Atticus draws the line and says no. "We still need Cal as much as we ever did," he says.

Jem urges Scout not to cause trouble for Atticus, who

is preoccupied with the Tom Robinson case. Scout feels Jem is talking down to her too much and they argue, ironically forcing Atticus to part them and send them to bed.

As Scout goes to her room, she steps on something that moves. Scout thinks it's a snake and fetches Jem. They discover it's actually Dill, who has run away from his parents and taken the bus to Maycomb. He feels they weren't giving him the love and attention he wanted. Jem, in trying to be a mature authority, tells Atticus that Dill is there. Scout views Jem's tattling on Dill as a great betrayal.

Atticus gets Dill properly fed and encourages a bath, and goes to tell Dill's aunt Rachel that the boy is there. Dill and Scout forgive Jem for ratting on them, but Dill is still uncomfortable with his foster family. He spends the night with the Finches and offers his perspective to Scout.

**CHAPTER 15:** Dill's foster family agrees to let Dill stay with the Finches for a while. Meanwhile, townsfolk are growing more perturbed with Atticus and his planned defense in court of Tom Robinson. Jem is worried when Atticus talks with a group of men on their lawn. It's unclear the actual danger Atticus is in, but their father assures them that he was just talking with their neighbors and friends. He may only be saying this to keep them calm, or he may actually believe that they are good people who won't do anything foolish.

Tom Robinson is moved to the Maycomb jail for his safety. One evening after he's been moved, Atticus informs the family that he's going out. He takes the car, something he doesn't usually do. Jem is uneasy and suspicious, and Scout and Dill accompany him downtown to discover what Atticus is up to. They find their father sitting with a light in front of the Maycomb jail. They are about to head home, when they see four cars drive up to the jail.

The men in the cars tell Atticus that they called the sheriff away on a false alarm so he wouldn't be at the jail. They want to kill Tom Robinson as a mob, but Atticus refuses to move. Unaware of the danger, Scout runs up and says hello to Atticus, who is suddenly worried that his children might get hurt. He tells them to go home. A man in the crowd tries to make the children leave. but Scout kicks him. Then she recognizes Walter Cunningham's father and starts to talk to him. He reluctantly speaks to her, then feels embarrassment for the situation and recognizes how Atticus helped him with his legal affairs. He calls the men off and they depart.

Atticus is clearly rattled by the whole experience. From inside the jail, the voice of Tom Robinson inquires if the men are gone. He has heard it all.

From the office of the Maycomb Tribune newspaper, the voice of Mr. Underwood, its editor, tells Atticus that he was keeping an eye on the men with his shotgun the whole time, underscoring the intensity of the moment.

Atticus and the children walk home. Instead of criticizing their decision to come downtown, he shows his affection and gratitude.

**CHAPTER 16:** They quietly enter the house so as not to wake Aunt Alexandra. There is a growing tension between Atticus and his sister. Alexandra views the blacks in the community as people separate from the whites. She sympathizes with them, but doesn't feel that genteel white people should associate with them. She views the trouble of the previous night as a necessary outcome of Atticus's actions. "You see what comes of things like this," she tells him.

The children then give a commentary on the people heading to the courthouse to watch Tom Robinson's trial. They are an idiosyncratic group of townsfolk, some rather close-minded, but all unique to look upon. Miss Maudie Atkinson won't be going to the trial. She says it's morbid and compares the event to a Roman carnival. A jury is picked for the trial that morning.

A man named Dolphus Raymond is described by Jem to Dill. Jem says, "He's got a colored woman and all sorts of mixed chillun." Along with his supposed drinking habit, this makes Raymond an outcast to both white and black society. Dill wonders how people can tell if Raymond's children are black or white, reminding us that a lot of what Maycomb residents see as "race" only exists in their minds. Later in the book, Dolphus Raymond will actually talk with the children and we'll see that's he's not just a drunk.

The children rush to the courtroom to get good seats. It's very crowded and they can't get a good view in the lower section where the white people sit. Reverend Sykes from Calpurnia's church invites them to the upper floor seats where the blacks sit, and they can see better up there.

The jury members look like farmers to Scout. She thinks that one of them looks like a Cunningham.

The case will be tried by Judge Taylor. The first witness is already on the stand: Sheriff Heck Tate.

**CHAPTER 17:** Mr. Gilmer, the prosecutor for the state, interviews Heck Tate first. He explains how Bob Ewell took him to his house on November 21 of the previous year to pick up Tom Robinson for raping his daughter. When Atticus interviews Tate, he makes it clear that nobody bothered to call for a doctor to examine Mayella Ewell. We also learn that Mayella's right side was more beaten up, as though hit by a left-handed man.

The next witness examined is Bob Ewell. Scout describes where the Ewells live: behind the town garbage dump. She isn't sure how many children are out there, but it's made clear that they live a pretty squalid existence. Bob Ewell says he came home to find his daughter screaming and being raped by Tom Robinson. (At this point, Reverend Sykes tries to send the children home, but they won't budge) Ewell says that Robinson fled, and then Ewell went to get the sheriff.

Atticus begins to interview the witness and again wonders why nobody called a doctor for Mayella. Then he asks if Ewell can write, and to verify this Atticus supplies a pen and paper. Everyone notices that Ewell writes with his left hand.

**CHAPTER 18:** Mayella Ewell is next called to give testimony. She claims that she only called Tom Robinson into the house to do some work, and that he took advantage of her and raped her.

When Atticus interviews her, Mayella thinks he is making fun of her by referring to her as "ma'am" and "Miss Mayella." Her life has been so rough that she's never had anyone speak to her politely. The judge assures her Atticus isn't mocking her.

Atticus paints a picture of her life in that house. "Who are your friends?" he asks, and she isn't able to come up with any. When he comes to Tom Robinson's actions, particularly his supposed beating, she goes back and forth before settling on what Robinson actually did. She is finally asked to identify Tom, and when he stands up it is clear his left arm is damaged from an accident. Reverend Sykes tells the children, "He got it caught in a cotton gin, caught it in Mr. Dolphus Raymond's cotton gin when he was a boy..." It seems unlikely that he hit Mayella on that side of her face as she describes.

Realizing she's painted herself into a corner and that Atticus's reasoning is too concise for her, Mayella reverts to emotion and tries to get the town on her side by saying, "That nigger yonder took advantage of me an' if you fine fancy gentlemen don't wanta do nothin' about it then you're all yellow stinkin' cowards, stinkin' cowards, the lot of you."

It's about four p.m. now, and Atticus calls his only witness: Tom Robinson.

**CHAPTER 19:** Tom Robinson is the last witness. He works in the fields of Link Deas and passed the Ewell house regularly. He claims Mayella often asked him to do small chores for her, and that he never charged her any money. One day, she called him into the house to help and then she started squeezing him and kissing him. At that point, Bob Ewell saw them through the window and called Mayella a whore. Tom Robinson ran away and was later arrested by Heck Tate. He completely denies raping (or attempting to rape) Mayella.

When Mr. Gilmer interviews Tom, he tries to paint a different perspective. He makes it sound like Tom was waiting for the chance to rape Mayella. When he asks why Tom didn't charge money to do her chores, Tom says, "I felt right sorry for her," and this is a big mistake, for a black man to pity a white woman.

As the interview goes on, Dill starts to cry. Scout and Dill go outside to let him recover. Dill explains that he just couldn't stand the unfair interrogation tactics Mr. Gilmer was using on Tom Robinson. As he explains, they are interrupted by Dolphus Raymond, who says, "You aren't thin-hided, it just makes you sick, doesn't it?"

**CHAPTER 20:** Scout and Dill talk with Dolphus Raymond and learn that he isn't actually drunk all the time. He only pretends to be. He's not racist the way most people are, and they wouldn't understand him being with a black woman, so he pretends to be drunk.

They run back to the courtroom when Dill is feeling a little better. Atticus is giving his closing remarks to the jury. He presents a strong case for Tom Robinson's innocence, and implies that Bob Ewell is the real abuser of Mayella. Atticus points out the hypocrisy of the situation. The whole situation has been allowed to come to trial only because Ewell is white and Tom Robinson is black.

As readers, it seems clear what the jury must do, and Tom Robinson's acquittal seems likely. But we must remember that this is another era.

Calpurnia suddenly appears at the end of this section, to everyone's surprise.

**CHAPTER 21:** Calpurnia is there because she can't find Jem and Scout. When Atticus locates them in the upper balcony with the black people, he sends them home for supper. They beg to return for the verdict, and he gives in and allows it. They are excited and Jem expects Tom Robinson to be acquitted. Reverend Sykes says to him, "Now don't you be so confident, Mr. Jem. I ain't ever seen any jury decide in favor of a colored man over a white man..."

After a good delay the jury returns and reads the verdict of guilty. Atticus is resigned and doesn't show too much emotion, but Jem is crushed.

As Atticus leaves the courtroom, the blacks stand up and say, "Miss Jean Louise, stand up. Your father's passin'." Even though he was unable to free Tom

Robinson, they hold Atticus in the highest respect.

**CHAPTER 22:** Jem cries at the unfairness of it all as they catch up with Atticus in the street. Atticus agrees that it's not right, but says, "We're not through yet. There'll be an appeal, you can count on that."

They're surprised when they arrive home to discover that many black people have sent them food as gifts of gratitude. Atticus asks Calpurnia to tell them never to do it again — after all, they are in the middle of the Depression.

Miss Maudie Atkinson tries to console the children and helps them see how much Atticus has done. "...Atticus won't win, he can't win, but he's the only man in these parts who can keep a jury out so long in a case like that. And I thought to myself, well, we're making a step — it's just a baby-step, but it's a step."

To add insult to injury over the lost trial, Bob Ewell sees Atticus near the post office the next day, spits in his face, and tells him that he'll "get him" if it takes the rest of his life. There is a foreboding feeling that the family tribulations aren't yet over.

**CHAPTER 23:** Perhaps Bob Ewell was expecting a fight from Atticus. Instead Atticus only says that he is too old to fight. The children are concerned for their father and want him to carry a gun or do something to protect himself, but Atticus thinks Ewell's insult will be the end of it. Aunt Alexandra agrees with the children that Ewell has more planned.

They discuss the Robinson case some more and the possibility of an appeal. Both Atticus and Jem recognize the unjustness of the legal system, allowing people to be hung on circumstantial evidence. It is particular prejudiced against the blacks. Atticus says, "In our courts, when it's a white man's word against a black man's, the white man always wins. They're ugly, but those are the facts of life." To make matters worse, townsfolk rarely sit on juries, and women never sit on juries in Alabama at that time.

When the jury selection took place, one of the Cunninghams was actually selected. Atticus could have rejected him, but chose not to. It was a risk, but the man almost gave a "not guilty" verdict. Jem has newfound respect for Walter Cunningham, but Aunt Alexandra says that the Cunninghams are not to be associated with, that they're a different kind of people from them. Jem and Scout puzzle over this until Scout concludes: "Naw, Jem, I think there's just one kind of folks. Folks." Scout is able to see people more humanely and fairly than many adults in the town.

**CHAPTER 24:** The end of another summer approaches. Dill prepares to leave. Before he goes, Jem takes him down to Barker's Eddy to teach him how to swim. Scout is home with Aunt Alexandra and her women guests. They're discussing the Tom Robinson case and its aftermath. The women talk about the black community in a condescending way. Ironically, they're also talking about helping the poor people in Africa, ignoring the injustice in their own backyard. Miss Maudie Atkinson is there and she mocks the other women's self-righteousness.

Atticus arrives home and asks Calpurnia to go to the house of Helen Robinson, Tom Robinson's wife. He says that Tom was shot while trying to escape from prison. He just ran and they shot him seventeen times. Atticus wants Calpurnia to come with him to break the news to Helen that her husband is dead.

Atticus and Calpurnia leave. Scout, Maudie, and Alexandra remain to have food and drink with the ladies.

They are deeply affected by the news of Tom's death, but they do their best to put on a good face. This ability to keep cool and well-mannered is something Scout is learning from the women.

**CHAPTER 25:** Scout is annoyed that Jem has entered a new phase of his existence wherein he values all animal life and refuses to kill a bug. This makes her miss Dill, who has left now that summer is over. She recalls that Jem taught Dill to swim in his final days in Maycomb. While coming home, Jem and Dill caught a ride from Atticus and Calpurnia (who were on their way to Helen Robinson's to tell her of her husband's death). Jem and Dill witness Helen's anguish when she hears the news.

Mr. Underwood writes a bitter editorial about Tom Robinson's death. Scout says, "[He] simply figured it was a sin to kill cripples, be they standing, sitting, or escaping."

When Bob Ewell heard of Tom Robinson's death, he supposedly said "it made one down and about two more to go." These other two would be Judge Taylor and Atticus. Jem hears Miss Stephanie say this, but he orders Scout not to say anything about it to Atticus. It would only disturb him further.

**CHAPTER 26:** Back in school, Scout reflects on the passage of time, her own maturity, and how she views the Radley residence differently now. She's not frightened of it, but it's still inhospitable, and she remains curious about Boo Radley, who she's sure is still inside.

Scout's teacher Miss Gates tells the children about Adolf Hitler, whose power in Germany had grown enormously at that time. She says that Hitler is persecuting the Jews and that it's very unfair.

Scout later hears Miss Gates talking about the blacks in the community in a way as racist as anyone else. Scout hears Miss Gates say that "it's time somebody taught 'em a lesson, they were gettin' way above themselves, an' the next thing they think they can do is marry us."

Scout asks Jem about it, and the mere mention of the courthouse angers him. She mentions this to Atticus, who tells her Jem needs time to sort something out within him, and eventually he will come to himself again. Scout will also have to sort some things out for herself as she enters the contradictory and confusing world of adults.

**CHAPTER 27:** By mid-October a few things have happened related to previous events in the story. First, Bob Ewell held a job for a few days and was then fired. Second, Judge Taylor heard a sound and saw a shadow outside his house one evening. Harper Lee is foreshadowing that Bob Ewell will do something, that he is seething with resentment for Atticus and all who embarrassed him at Tom Robinson's trial.

Ewell has caused trouble for Robinson's widow Helen. Every day, Helen walks a mile further than she needs to so she'll avoid Ewell's house on her way to work. When her employer (Link Deas) learns of this, he accompanies her on the shorter route and verbally chastises Ewell, who doesn't bother Helen after that.

As Halloween approaches, Scout is enlisted to take part in a pageant. Her costume will portray a ham, one of Maycomb County's agricultural products. However, nobody seems to want to take her to the pageant. She shows off her part to Atticus and Aunt Alexandra in the living room, but only Jem accompanies her to the school. We have more foreshadowing that something dramatic will occur. As Scout prepares to leave, she narrates: "Thus began our longest journey together."

**CHAPTER 28:** Jem and Scout pass the Radley house on their way to the pageant. There's a spooky atmosphere. When they get near the school auditorium, someone jumps out and startles them. It is Cecil Jacobs. He and Scout put their costumes behind the stage and go off to explore the carnival amusements, while Jem goes to be with people his own age.

Most of Maycomb seems to be there that night. The pageant takes place – for the most part Scout is bored.

Jem and Scout walk home and think they hear someone following them. Scout thinks it's Cecil Jacobs trying to surprise them again. It's very dark and they can't be sure. In the darkness, someone tries to grab them. They scream and Jem is hurt. It is very confusing for the children.

Atticus and others arrive and carry Jem back to their house. Heck Tate (the sheriff) is phoned. Everyone is trying to determine what happened. Scout fears that Jem might be dead, but that doesn't seem to be the case.

Heck Tate arrives and investigates. There is also a man in their house who Scout doesn't recognize. Heck Tate goes back to the scene of the attack to see what happened, and discovers Bob Ewell dead. He says, "Bob Ewell's lyin' on the ground under that tree down yonder with a kitchen knife stuck up under his ribs. He's dead, Mr. Finch."

**CHAPTER 29:** Jem has a broken arm (the incident referred to in the very first sentence of the novel). He rests while the family and sheriff discuss what happened. They examine the costume Scout wore and realize that it protected her from Bob Ewell's knife. She relates what she remembers: Somebody – Bob Ewell she now realizes – grabbed for her and Jem, but then someone else pulled

Mr. Ewell down. They ask who it was, and she points to the stranger in their house. As she examines the man, she realizes it is Boo Radley, finally revealed to her at last. "Hey, Boo," she says.

**CHAPTER 30:** The sheriff and Atticus further discuss what has occurred. Atticus believes that Jem forced Bob Ewell into his own knife, killing him, and refuses to keep his son from the process of the law. Heck Tate, on the other hand, tells Atticus that Jem couldn't have possibly been at fault in Ewell's death. He says that Ewell fell on his own knife, and that's the end of it. Both men are stubborn, but Atticus finally gives in. Heck Tate then implies that the real person responsible for Ewell's death is Boo Radley. But he refuses to bring Boo into the public light like that – he has helped the children, and to torture him with public scrutiny would do a service to no one. So for all intents and purposes, Bob Ewell fell on his own knife.

Atticus tries to explain this to Scout, and she says, "Well, it'd be sort of like shootin' a mockingbird, wouldn't it?" Once again, Scout has demonstrated that she sees deeper into things than many adults do.

**CHAPTER 31:** Boo and Scout share a quiet understanding as they observe Jem sleeping. Scout encourages Boo to pat Jem's head. Boo then says his only words in the novel: "Will you take me home?"

Scout walks Boo home, and then tells us that was the last time she ever saw Boo Radley.

As Scout walks down her street, she reflects on all that has taken place there, all that continues to take place as people carry in life through their patterns and habits, changing and growing.

At home she finds Atticus reading *The Gray Ghost*, one of Jem's books. She asks her father to read it to her and he does for a while until she is too drowsy to stay awake. She comments on the main character in the book being nice, and Atticus says, "Most people are, Scout, when you finally see them."

This of course refers to Boo Radley, but also to all the people in the book, and the barriers put in place to keep them from seeing that.

Atticus returns to Jem's room. He stays there all night keeping watch on his son, and the book concludes.

# CRITICAL QUESTIONS & ESSAY TOPICS

Here are some critical questions and essay topics about the book. These questions may be answered in a variety of ways based on your reading of the text. I have provided suggestions in the answers below, but I encourage you to consider alternative answers as you explore these topics.

**1. Atticus is often presented as a moral compass and role model for the children. Does he make any poor choices in the novel?**

Atticus isn't perfect. He makes several poor choices in the book. For example, he tries to make Scout and Jem more genteel than is necessary. But he can also admit when he has done wrong, and makes a genuine attempt to make amends. He strives to improve and be his best, and that – not an artificial perfection – is what makes him an admirable character.

**2. Why does Aunt Alexandra come to stay with the family?**

More than any need to make the children well-mannered, Aunt Alexandra's presence adds a layer of protection to the Finch house. Many people are unhappy Atticus is defending Tom Robinson. But to attack a household with a genteel lady would be against the code of Maycomb society.

## 3. How do Jem and Scout change through the story?

Jem goes through puberty and learns to accept that the world isn't always fair. He also learns that force can't solve every problem, and that courage takes many forms.

Scout doesn't go through the same *physical* maturity as Jem, but she does start to integrate into society. At the beginning of the book, she has never been to school. She also sees black people in a new light because of her experiences. She learns that violence isn't a long-term solution to her problems.

## 4. Are Jem and Scout typical children? Why are why not?

Jem and Scout seem both atypical in both intelligence and independence. We should remember that they only have one parent around, forcing them to do many things without supervision. They also have a different perspective of the town because of their father's radical actions and opinions. These things combine to make them seem relatively peculiar to children their age.

## 5. What is Atticus's parenting style?

Atticus is very busy as a lawyer. He often has no time for parenting as such. When he is around, his primary goal is to set a good example. He does not talk down to his children, and he listens to them carefully.

## 6. How is Maycomb depicted in the novel?

Maycomb is shown as a tight-knit community. People depend on each other, and hospitality is key. Due to this tight connection, there is little opportunity for thoughts and actions that go against community norms. People like Bob Ewell are ostracized. That being said, there are dissenters in the community, and people like Atticus, Maudie Atkinson, Dolphus Raymond, and others represent forward thinking.

### 7. Does Lee present a fair picture of race and class?

In terms of race, Lee depicts the black community as uniformly good and innocent. This may not be wholly representational, but it serves the purpose of the story. She is trying to humanize the black community, since many of the readers of her book were (and are) white.

Class distinctions are numerous in the book. The Ewells, the Cunninghams, and the Finches each exist on a specific social level, and the boundaries between the levels are firm for adults. Younger people like Scout and Dill are less concerned about class distinctions.

### 8. If Tom Robinson's innocence is as apparent to the jury as it is to us, why is he found guilty?

This is the great injustice of the book. Evil sometimes wins, and by reading the book we gain an awareness of what work remains to be done.

### 9. How has the lack of a mother affected Jem and Scout?

Without a mother, Calpurnia has had a large part in raising Jem and Scout. Other women like Maudie Atkinson and Aunt Alexandra have also taken a hand in raising them and serving as role models. That being said, there is probably an emotional loss felt by the children (especially Jem, who is older and remembers his mother).

### 10. Describe the relationship between Atticus

**and Aunt Alexandra.**

Atticus and Alexandra greatly respect each other, and Atticus appreciates his sister's help with his children. But when it comes down to it, Atticus is the parental figure who says how his children are to be raised.

## 11. Why does Boo leave items in the tree for the children?

Boo clearly wants to communicate with the children, but his reclusive nature makes this difficult. When he finally speaks to Scout, it's not much in the way of conversation. Leaving gifts in the tree is his best attempt at communication.

## 12. Why do you think this book has proven so popular?

The book was almost immediately popular. It was picked up by book groups and school planners. The movie release in 1962 further added to its popularity. I think the characters are the main reason for the book's popularity. It has a memorable cast and important lessons that we're still trying to resolve.

# CONCLUSION

*To Kill a Mockingbird* is a modern classic, as popular today as when it was first released. Its characters remain beloved in modern literature, and its lessons are still being absorbed by each generation that reads it. I hope this guide has helped you navigate this book, and deepened your understanding of all that occurs in its pages.

Printed in Great Britain
by Amazon

77616533R00029